Symbols of Freedom

National Parks

Grand Canyon National Park

M.C. Hall

Heinemann Library
Chicago, Illinois

Page layout by Richard Parker and Maverick Design
Photo research by Maria Joannou
Illustrations by Jeff Edwards
Printed and bound in China by South China Printing Company Limited

10
10 9 8 7 6 5 4 3

Library of Congress Cataloging-in-Publication Data
Hall, Margaret, 1947-
   Grand Canyon National Park / Margaret Hall.
      p. cm. -- (National parks)
Includes bibliographical references and index.
ISBN 1-4034-6699-8 (library binding-hardcover) -- ISBN 1-4034-6706-4 (pbk.)
ISBN 978-1-4034-6699-0 (library binding-hardcover) -- ISBN 978-1-4034-6706-5 (pbk.)
1. Grand Canyon National Park (Ariz.)--Juvenile literature. 2. Grand Canyon (Ariz.)--Juvenile literature.
I. Title. II. Series.
   F788.H225 2005
   979.1'32--dc22

                                    2004030338

Acknowledgments
The author and publishers are grateful to the following for permission to reproduce copyright material:
Corbis pp. **4**, **13**, **8** (Buddy Mays), **25** (Galen Rowell), **24** (James Randklev), **9** (John K. Hillers), **19** (Kevin Fleming), **20**, **27** (Tom Bean); Creatas/Dynamic Graphics p. **18** (John Foxx); Getty Images/ Stone pp. **7**, **14** (Cameron Davidson), **15** (Paul Edmondson), **17** (Tom Bean); National Park Service pp. **11**, **12**, **16**, **21**, **26**, **29**, **30**, **31**, **32**; Naturepl p. **23** (Huw Cordey); NHPA p. **22** (Daniel Heuclin); Topham Picturepoint p. **10**

Cover photograph of the Grand Canyon reproduced with permission of Robert Harding Picture Library (Tony Gervis)

Every effort has been made to contact copyright holders of any material reproduced in this book.
Any omissions will be rectified in subsequent printings if notice is given to the publisher.

Some words are shown in bold, **like this**. You can find out what they mean by looking in the glossary.

Contents

National parks are areas set aside for people to visit and enjoy **nature**. The land in national parks is protected. People cannot cut down trees or pick plants in a national park.

National Parks belong to all the people.

There are more than 50 national parks in the United States. Grand Canyon National Park is one of the most popular parks. Millions of people from around the world come to visit.

Grand Canyon National Park

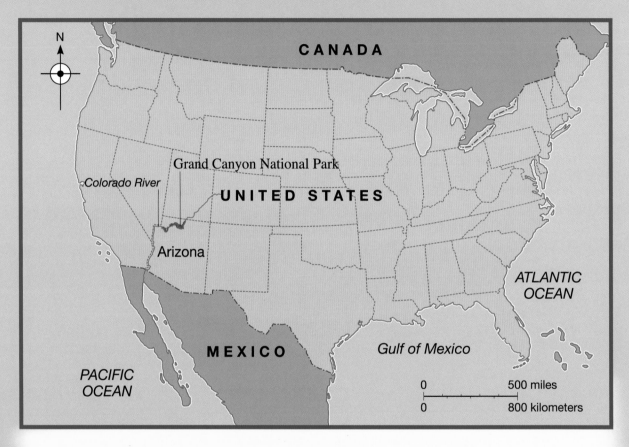

Grand Canyon National Park is in the northwest corner of Arizona. The Colorado River flows through the park. For millions of years, the river has worn away the rocks. It has formed a deep **canyon**.

Grand Canyon National Park gets its name from this canyon. The Grand Canyon is one of the largest canyons in the world.

This photo was taken from an airplane flying high above the canyon.

Thousands of years ago, Native Americans lived in and near the Grand Canyon. One group of Pueblo Indians built homes of mud bricks in the **canyon**. In 1540, a group of Spanish explorers visited the canyon.

These food storage areas may have been built by the Anasazi **tribe**.

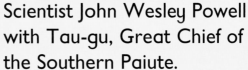
Scientist John Wesley Powell with Tau-gu, Great Chief of the Southern Paiute.

In 1869 John Wesley Powell came to explore the Grand Canyon. Later, other people came to see the canyon and river. In 1919 the United States **government** made the Grand Canyon a **national park**.

 # Visiting Grand Canyon National Park

If you visit the Grand Canyon in winter, you may see it covered in snow.

Grand Canyon National Park is open all year. However, most people visit in the summer. The weather is sunny and it is easy to get a clear view of the **canyon**.

Visitors enjoy seeing the canyon from the **rim**. Some people hike or ride mules to the bottom. Others get a great view from helicopters or small planes that fly over the canyon.

The Canyon

The Grand Canyon is so deep in some places that people standing at the top cannot see all the way to the bottom!

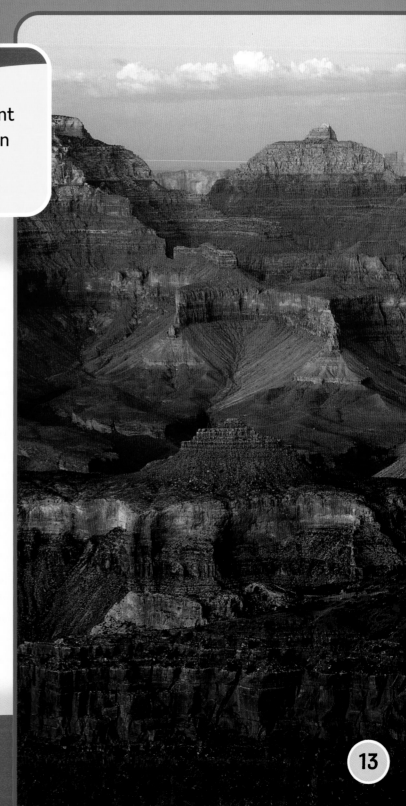

You can see the different colored layers of rock in this picture.

The walls of the Grand Canyon are made of layers of rock. These rocks are red, gray, green, pink, brown, and purple. Some layers have **fossils** of animals and plants that lived long ago.

The Canyon Rim

The south side of the **canyon** is the South Rim. There is a road here where visitors can stop at **overlooks** to view the canyon. They can also hike on trails that go along the **rim**.

overlook on South Rim

North Rim

The North Rim is higher and cooler than the South Rim. This part of the park is closed in the winter because of the snow. Summer visitors can hike and camp near the canyon.

Inside the Canyon

There are no roads to the bottom of the **canyon**. Long trails go from the **rim** to the canyon floor. The trails are steep and winding.

People can hike or ride horses and mules to the bottom of the canyon. Some campers take equipment and stay overnight on the canyon floor.

It gets very hot at the bottom of the canyon.

The River

The Colorado River starts in Colorado. It flows through the Grand Canyon on its way to Mexico. Many visitors come to **raft** on the river.

the Colorado River

Rafting down the Colorado River is exciting!

In some places the river is calm. Then the **canyon** gets narrow. The water flows very quickly around rocks in the river. Everyone on the rafts gets wet!

Grand Canyon Plants

Forests of tall ponderosa pines grow on both sides of the Grand Canyon. Spruce trees only grow on the North Rim, where the land is higher. Fewer trees grow along the dry South Rim.

The claretcup cactus grows where it is dry.

Several kinds of cactus grow in and around the **canyon**. There are also yucca plants, sagebrush, and twisted piñon trees.

Grand Canyon Animals

Many animals live in and near the **canyon**. Bighorn sheep climb the rocky canyon wall. There are also deer, coyotes, and mountain lions.

bighorn sheep

22

Small animals such as lizards, squirrels, and snakes live in the park. There are also many birds. The largest birds are the condor and the bald eagle.

chuckwalla lizard

The Havasupai get their name from the color of the water.

Today, the Havasupai **tribe** is a group of Native Americans living in the Grand Canyon. The tribe's name means "People of the Blue-Green Water."

The Havasupai people raise crops and animals. Some also work as guides and show visitors around their village and the park.

The Havasupai village is next to Grand Canyon National Park.

Park Buildings and People

There are three visitor centers in Grand Canyon National Park. There are also shops, a post office, and a bank at Grand Canyon Village, on the South Rim.

People learn about the park at the visitor centers.

Park rangers work in all parts of the park. The rangers teach visitors about the plants and animals of the Grand Canyon. They also lead hikes on the park's many trails.

Map of Grand Canyon National Park

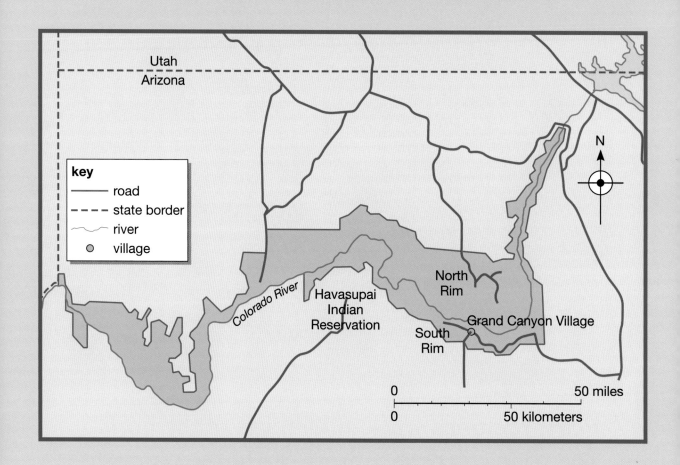

Utah
Arizona

key
— road
- - - state border
~~~ river
◉ village

Colorado River

Havasupai Indian Reservation

North Rim

South Rim

Grand Canyon Village

N

| 0 | | 50 miles |

| 0 | | 50 kilometers |

Timeline

4,000 *years ago*   Native Americans live in and around the Grand Canyon

1540   Spanish explorer Garcia Lopez de Cárdenas is the first **European** to see the Grand Canyon

1869   John Wesley Powell and a team of men explore the Grand Canyon

1919   The Grand Canyon becomes a **national park**

1936   Hoover **Dam** is completed on the Colorado River outside the park

1938   The first **commercial raft** trip through the Grand Canyon

1964   Glen Canyon Dam is completed on the Colorado River

1975   The area of the park is enlarged

1979   The park becomes a World Heritage Site

Glossary

canyon very steep valley

commercial made so that it can make money

dam wall built across a river to hold back water

European from Europe

fossil plant or animal that died millions of years ago and turned to stone

government group of people that makes laws for and runs a country

national park natural area set aside by the government for people to visit

nature the outdoors and the wild plants and animals found there

overlook place set aside for viewing something from above

park ranger man or woman who works in a national park and shares information about the wildlife and unusual sights of the park

raft floating platform used for moving things over water

rim upper edge

tribe Native American group

Find Out More

Books
An older reader can help you with these books:

Adams, Colleen. *Exploring the Grand Canyon.* New York, N.Y.: Rosen Publishing Group, Inc, 2002.

Graf, Mike. *Grand Canyon National Park.* Mankato, Minn.: Bridgestone Books, 2003.

Meister, Cari. *Grand Canyon.* Mankato, Minn.: ABDO Publishing Co, 2000.

Raatma, Lucia. *Our National Parks.* Mankato, Minn.: Compass Point Books, 2002.

Viera, Linda. *Grand Canyon.* New York, N.Y.: Walker and Company, 2000.

Weintraub, Aileen. *Grand Canyon: The Widest Canyon.* New York, N.Y.: PowerKids Press, 2001.

Address
To find out more about Grand Canyon National Park, write to:

Grand Canyon National Park
P.O. Box 129
Grand Canyon, AZ 86023

Index